THE
Fantastic
CUTAWAY BOOK OF
SPEED

JON RICHARDS *AND* ALEX PANG

COPPER BEECH BOOKS
BROOKFIELD, CONNECTICUT

CONTENTS

This edition published in
the United States in 1997
by
Copper Beech Books,
an imprint of
The Millbrook Press
2 Old New Milford Road
Brookfield, Connecticut
06804

Printed in Belgium

Editor
Simon Beecroft
Consultant
Steve Allman
Design
David West
Children's Book Design
Designer
Rob Perry
Picture research
Brooks Krikler Research
Illustrators Alex Pang
and Graham White

Library of Congress
Cataloging-in-Publication Data
Richards, Jon, 1970-
The fantastic cutaway book of
speed / by Jon Richards ;
illustrated by Alex Pang.
p. cm.
Includes index.
Summary: Captioned illustrations
provide information about some
of the world's fastest vehicles on
land, sea, and in the air and
describe recent record-setting
attempts.
ISBN 0-7613-0554-8 (lib. bdg.).
— ISBN 0-7613-0579-3
(trade pbk.)
1. Motor vehicles—Juvenile
literature. 2. Speed records–
–Juvenile literature.
3. Motorsports—Juvenile
literature. [1. Motor vehicles.
2. Speed records.] I. Pang, Alex,
ill. II. Title.

INTRODUCTION

Since the earliest days of powered transportation, people have always felt the desire to make their cars, boats, and planes go faster. In this quest for speed, designers and builders have continuously battled against the restricting forces of nature and physics, while the drivers and pilots themselves have risked their lives (and often lost them!) driving cars, steering boats, or flying planes – all in a constant search to find ways of pushing the performance of their vehicles beyond the existing limits.

The result has been the development of some amazing machines, all capable of reaching breathtaking speeds. These range from boats that can lift themselves out of the water and literally fly across its surface to cars powered by enormous jet and rocket engines, and planes that can scratch the very edge of space.

THE *MCLAREN F-1* is one of the most outstanding supercars ever built. It was designed using the technical skills of the McLaren motor racing team. Since its launch in 1992, the racing version, the *F-1 GTR* (below), has gone on to win the 24-hour endurance race at Le Mans and the Global Endurance GT Series. The road-going version, the *F-1 LM* (main picture), is no less thrilling to drive. It has a top speed of 225 mph (360 km/h) – making it one of the fastest cars on the road. It is able to accelerate from a standing start to 60 mph (96 km/h) in under three seconds, and it can reach 100 mph (160 km/h) in a little under five seconds!

McLaren F-1 LM

KEEPING LIGHT

The weight of the F-1 LM is kept down to only 2,336 lb (1,062 kg) due to the use of strong but light-weight materials in the car's construction, such as aluminum and carbon fiber. By combining a light-weight car with a powerful engine, the designers were able to ensure that the F-1 could accelerate at a phenomenal rate.

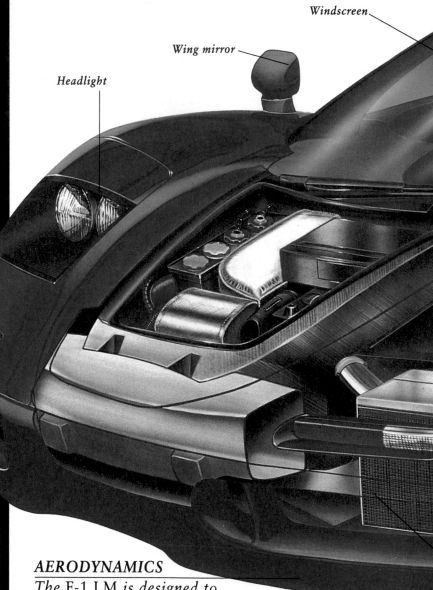

Windscreen

Wing mirror

Headlight

AERODYNAMICS

The F-1 LM is designed to slice through the air and yet stick to the road. Large fans on the bottom of the car suck air from underneath, increasing the downward force on the car. This, in effect, glues the car to the road, allowing it to take bends and corners with greater speed.

McLaren F-1 GTR

BMW MOTORSPORT ENGINE

ENGINE POWER
The F-1 is powered by a 372-cubic-inch (6.1-liter), V-12 BMW engine (left). At 7,800 revolutions per minute (rpm) it can deliver an amazing 668 brake horsepower (bhp).

THE
MCLAREN
F-1

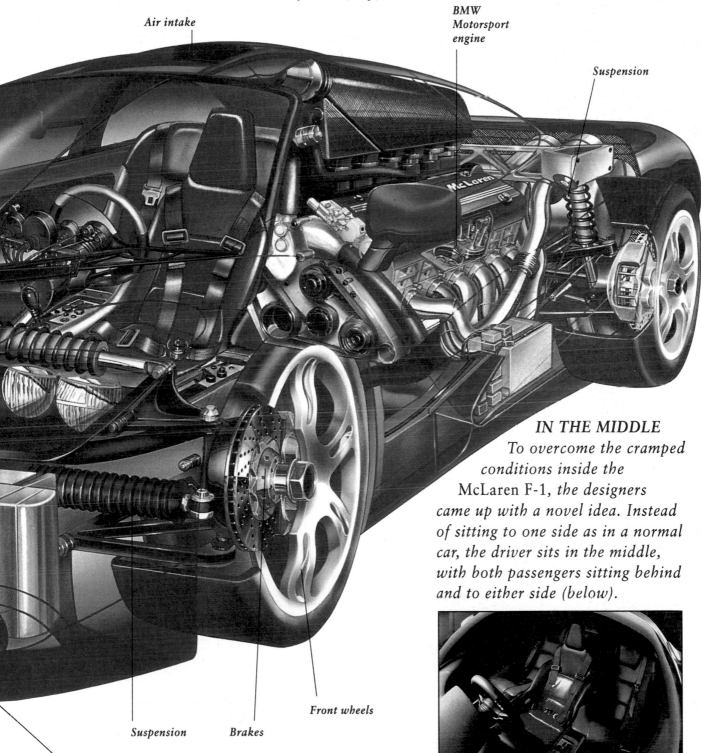

Air intake

BMW Motorsport engine

Suspension

IN THE MIDDLE
To overcome the cramped conditions inside the McLaren F-1, the designers came up with a novel idea. Instead of sitting to one side as in a normal car, the driver sits in the middle, with both passengers sitting behind and to either side (below).

Front wheels

Suspension   Brakes

Air ducts

DRIVER'S AND PASSENGERS' SEATS

ON THE ROAD

MERCEDES
300 SL
"GULLWING"

The period immediately before and after World War II is often described as the golden age for sporting road cars, such as the Auburn Speedster *and the* Jaguar XK 120. *The* Delahaye Type 135 *(left) was introduced in the late 1930s. Racing versions of this car had instant successes. Powered by a 214-cubic-inch (3.5-liter) engine, they won the Le Mans 24-hour race in 1938 as well as the Monte Carlo Rally twice, in 1937 and 1939.*

DELAHAYE
TYPE 135

JAGUAR E-TYPE

The E-type Jaguar *(below) not only looks fast, but goes fast too! It has a maximum speed of 150 mph (241 km/h) and an acceleration of 0-60 mph (0-96 km/h) in a little under seven seconds. Its sleek looks and stunning performance made the E-type one of the classic cars of the 1960s. A total of over 72,000 were built between 1961 and 1974.*

MERCEDES 300 SL "GULLWING"

The Mercedes 300 SL "Gullwing" *(above) gets its nickname from its unusual doors that open vertically rather than horizontally. It is derived from the racing car that won the 1952 Le Mans 24-hour race and was in production from 1954 to 1957.*

Because of its racing pedigree, the Gullwing has some impressive performance figures. The 183-cubic-inch (3-liter) engine can accelerate the car from 0–60 mph (0–96 km/h) in just over 8 seconds, and push it to speeds of up to 165 mph (265 km/h).

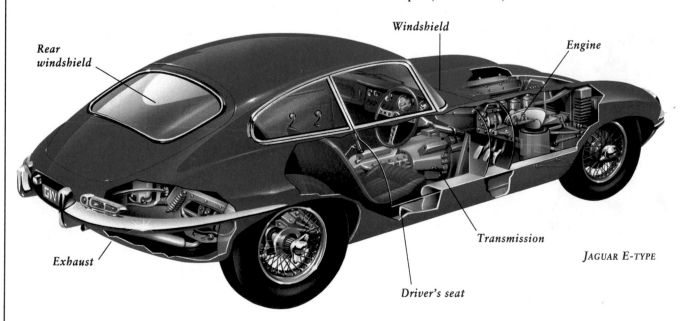

Rear windshield

Windshield

Engine

Transmission

Exhaust

Driver's seat

JAGUAR E-TYPE

AC COBRA 427

Built between 1965 and 1968, the AC Cobra 427 holds a massive 430-cubic-inch (7-liter) V-8 Ford Mustang engine. This produces 425 bhp and can drive the car to a maximum speed of 165 mph (265 km/h). It can also accelerate from 0–60 mph (0–96 km/h) in a mere 4.2 seconds – it used to hold the record as the world's fastest accelerating car!

AC COBRA

FERRARI 275 GTB/4

Only 350 of these powerful road cars (left) were built between 1966 and 1968.

FERRARI 275 GTB/4

Underneath the hood was a 201-cubic-inch (3.3-liter) V-12 engine that could deliver 300 bhp. This meant that the car could reach 160 mph (257 km/h) and accelerate from 0-60 mph (0-96 km/h) in an amazingly fast 5.5 seconds. The 275 paved the way for its successor, the Ferrari Daytona, which was the fastest car of its day with a top speed of 174 mph (280 km/h)!

PORSCHE 356

Despite being the 356th project to come from the Porsche design offices (hence the name), the 356 (below) was the first car to bear the Porsche name. Like its Porsche-designed predecessor, the Volkswagen Beetle, the 356's engine was in the rear of the car. This 98-cubic-inch (1.6-liter) engine could produce

PORSCHE 356

90 bhp, powering the car to a top speed of 110 mph (177 km/h).

JAGUAR XJ220

The Jaguar XJ220 (below) is truly a "supercar" – a car whose performance is far superior to normal road cars. Other cars in this class include the Lamborghini Diablo and the McLaren F1 (see pages 4-5). Launched in 1988, the XJ220 boasts a V-6, fuel-injected turbo engine (left) that can accelerate the car from 0-60 mph (0-96 km/h) in an amazing 3.75 seconds. It can also achieve a top speed of 212 mph (341 km/h)!.

V-6 JAGUAR ENGINE

JAGUAR XJ220

A PIT STOP DURING THE RACE

FORMULA ONE RACING

is an incredibly popular sport that draws huge audiences. They are attracted by the excitement of watching cars hurtle around tracks at top speed. Over the course of sixteen or seventeen races, the racing teams compete for the driver's and constructor's championship. Beyond these races, the teams are constantly developing and testing their cars. All of this is necessary to get the best from driver and machine in a sport where the smallest fraction of a second can be vital.

PIT STOPS

Pit stops (left) allow the car to refuel and replace its tires, and so maintain its peak performance. Once the car has come to a halt at the pit, at least seventeen mechanics work around the car, changing its tires, pumping fuel into the tank, and even changing damaged parts. All of this can be achieved in under 10 seconds.

SAFETY

Safety is paramount in Formula One racing. The drivers are strapped firmly into a very strong

RACE MARSHALLS EXAMINE A CRASHED CAR

cockpit. In a crash, this will remain intact while other parts of the car, such as the wheels, absorb the impact. Drivers are also covered in layers of fire-proof clothing and wear helmets that can protect against a stone catapulted at 313 mph (500 km/h).

The track itself is surrounded by crash barriers and walls of tires. Fire marshals are also stationed around the circuit and can reach a crashed vehicle within seconds of an incident (above).

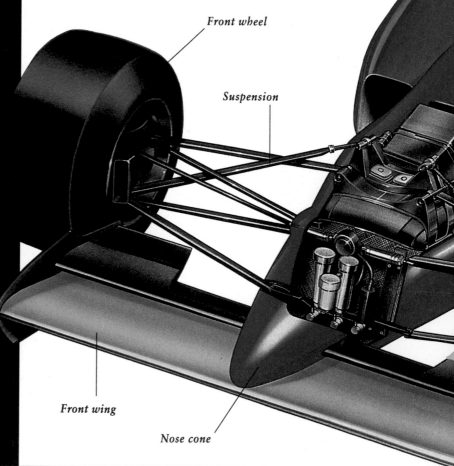

Front wheel

Suspension

Front wing

Nose cone

TIRES
There are two types of tire tread available for racing. One slick, treadless tire for dry weather conditions and one covered in a deep tread to use in the rain (above).

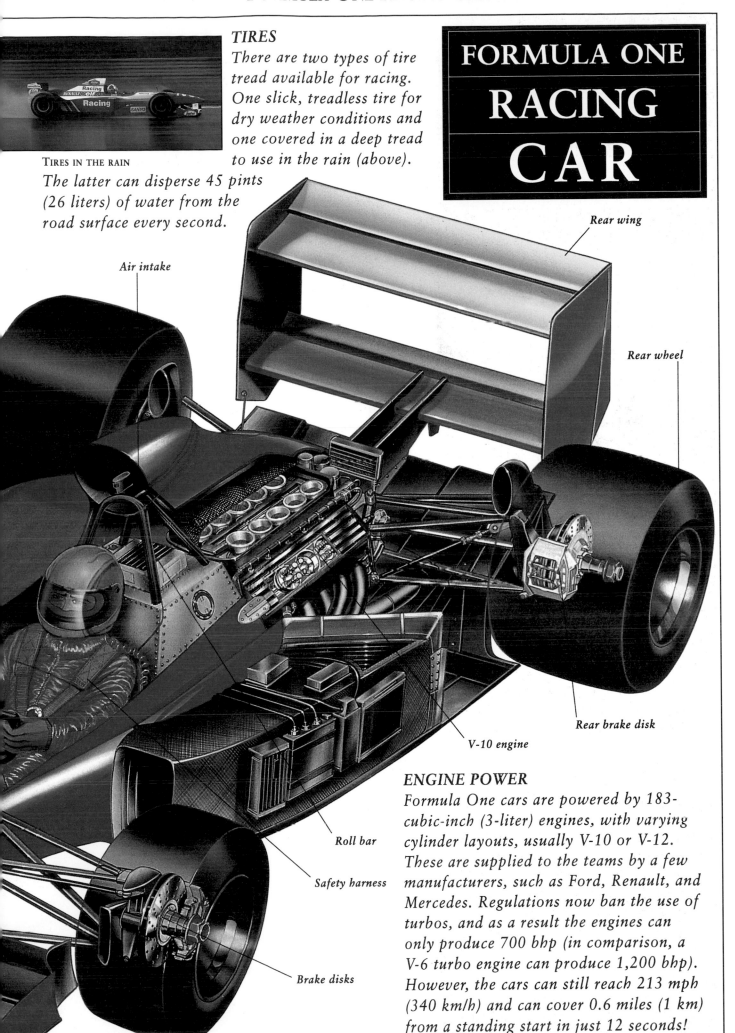

TIRES IN THE RAIN

The latter can disperse 45 pints (26 liters) of water from the road surface every second.

FORMULA ONE RACING CAR

Air intake

Rear wing

Rear wheel

Rear brake disk

V-10 engine

Roll bar

Safety harness

Brake disks

ENGINE POWER
Formula One cars are powered by 183-cubic-inch (3-liter) engines, with varying cylinder layouts, usually V-10 or V-12. These are supplied to the teams by a few manufacturers, such as Ford, Renault, and Mercedes. Regulations now ban the use of turbos, and as a result the engines can only produce 700 bhp (in comparison, a V-6 turbo engine can produce 1,200 bhp). However, the cars can still reach 213 mph (340 km/h) and can cover 0.6 miles (1 km) from a standing start in just 12 seconds!

RACING CARS

DRIVERS

During his career, Juan Fangio (left) won the world championship five times. He started in pole position a total of 28 times and won 24 races. One of the most successful drivers of modern times was Ayrton Senna (right). He started in pole position 65 times, won 41 grand prix, and won the world championship three times. Tragically, he was killed in 1994 while leading the San Marino Grand Prix at Imola.

JUAN FANGIO

AYRTON SENNA

During the early days of motor racing, cars were huge, front-engined machines – very different from the sleek cars that race today. The Sunbeam Tourist from 1914 had a front-mounted engine, with the driver sitting upright. Gradually, the shape of the cars' body changed, to produce a more streamlined effect. By the 1950s, in cars such as the Mercedes-Benz W196 and the Type 158 Alfa Romeo, the drivers were sitting lower and behind much more powerful engines.

1914 SUNBEAM TOURIST

1950 ALFA ROMEO 158

During the next decades, the engine was moved to the back. Monocoque chassis (where the engine forms part of the chassis as opposed to sitting inside one) were introduced, and wings were used to increase the downforce on the car. All of these features were used in the Matra that Jackie Stewart drove in 1969. The 1973 McLaren-Ford shows how the radiator moved from the front of the car to its sides, allowing for a greater aerodynamic nose.

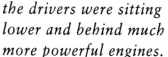

1954 MERCEDES W196

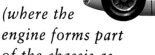

1969 MATRA

1973 McLAREN-FORD

INNOVATIONS

A constant battle exists between car designers who want to build a car to go as fast as possible, and the sport's lawmakers who want to keep a car's performance within safe limits. Many innovations have been banned. The Chaparral 2E (above) had large wings that were used to improve the car's grip on the road.

Since 1969, the wings' size has been limited. Six-wheeled cars, such as the Tyrrel P34 (right), were banned in 1976.

CHAPARRAL 2E

TYRREL P34

INDY CAR

Indy cars (right) have a powerful V-8 turbo-charged engine, which produces 800 bhp, pushing the car at speeds of up to 213 mph (340 km/h). Indy races are often held on oval circuits that have banked corners. To cope with these banked curves the driver can elevate one side of the car using compressed air. Every year, the Indianapolis 500 is held at the world's oldest racetrack, the 2.5-mile (4-km) long "Brickyard."

INDY CAR

BENTLEY NAPIER

LE MANS

The Le Mans 24-hour race was first held in 1923. Teams raced to see who could drive the farthest during a night and a day around a 8.6-mile (13.5-km) circuit. In the early days, the race was started by the drivers running across the track to their cars. Today, the cars line up behind a slow-moving pace car. When the pace car moves aside, the race begins. This is called a rolling start (above).

LE MANS ROLLING START

MONTE CARLO RALLY

This unique race was first run in 1911 and has been held nearly every year since, except during the two World Wars and the gasoline crisis of 1974. During the race, hundreds of rally drivers race to Monte Carlo from starting points in Europe and Africa. Weather conditions have always proved a key factor. So much so, that in the winter of 1965 only 22 cars finished out of the 237 that started.

MONTE CARLO RALLY

FORD GT40

The Ford GT40 (above) was introduced to the Le Mans 24-hour race in 1964. The car was powered by a 305-cubic-inch (5-liter) engine and was capable of 164 mph (264 km/h). The GT40 failed in its first two attempts to win before taking first place in 1966. It then asserted its dominance on the track by winning the race for the next three years.

FORD GT40

NASCAR

National Association for Stock Car Auto Racing (NASCAR) is a form of racing popular in the United States. Stock cars speed around paved oval tracks with banked corners. Crashes are common, as cars jostle for position during the race.

NASCAR RACING

BURNING RUBBER

ENGINE POWER

Beneath the hood of a Funny Car dragster sits an extremely powerful 500-cubic-inch (8.2-liter) supercharged engine. Supplying this is a fuel pump that can deliver about 50 gallons (225 liters) of fuel (either nitromethane or an alcohol and methanol mix) each minute. This means that during a five-second run, a dragster will use 15 gallons (65 liters) of fuel!

Safety cage

Driver

Rear spoiler

Rear wheel

Rear axle

DRIVER SAFETY

The dragster is fitted with an automatic fire extinguisher system. The driver has to wear a flame-proof suit with helmet, head sock, and a neck collar.

SINCE ITS EARLY DAYS in the 1930s, hot rodding, or drag racing as it is now known, has grown into a worldwide sport. During a race, incredibly fast cars hurtle down a straight track that is 0.25 miles (0.4 km) long. Today, the fastest of these vehicles can complete the run in a little under five seconds!

So-called Funny Cars (main picture) are slightly slower than their stripped-down cousins, the Top Fuel dragsters (right). However, they use an identical engine to the Top Fuel cars (see top of page) and can still reach speeds of 290 mph (466 km/h). They are also fitted with a parachute to help slow them down.

FUNNY CAR
DRAGSTER

FUNNY CAR DRAGSTER

SUPERCHARGER

Sitting on top of the engine is a supercharger (right). This device is driven mechanically by the engine and sucks in an enormous amount of extra air. This extra air is forced into the cylinders, where it raises the pressure of the fuel and air mix. This gives the engine a massive and immediate surge of power.

SUPERCHARGED ENGINE

Engine

Front wheel

Fuel tank

TOP FUEL DRAGSTER

LIGHTWEIGHT BODY

The chassis of the Funny Car is surrounded by a body made from lightweight carbon fiber. The weight of the whole car has to be kept to a minimum to help it accelerate as quickly as possible. This acceleration is so great that the dragster is fitted with a wheelie bar at the rear to stop the car from flipping over.

GRAND PRIX RACING BIKE

Windscreen

Kevlar-reinforced carbon fiber bodywork

Exhaust

Rear wheel

Exhaust

RIDER SAFETY

As with its four-wheeled cousin, motorcycle racing is not without a certain amount of danger (below). To reduce the risks to the rider, they wear sturdy leather outfits and crash helmets. Today's crash helmets are made from fiberglass and plastic. Before current specifications, helmets were made from canvas, cork, and leather and only covered the top of the skull, giving no protection to the sides of the head.

GRAND PRIX CRASH

KNEE-DOWN CORNERING

Fast corners are usually taken with the rider adopting a "knee-down" position (below). This involves the rider scraping a knee against the track as he leans into the turn. To help him through the corner the rider wears special knee pads covered with hard-wearing, solid-nylon patches.

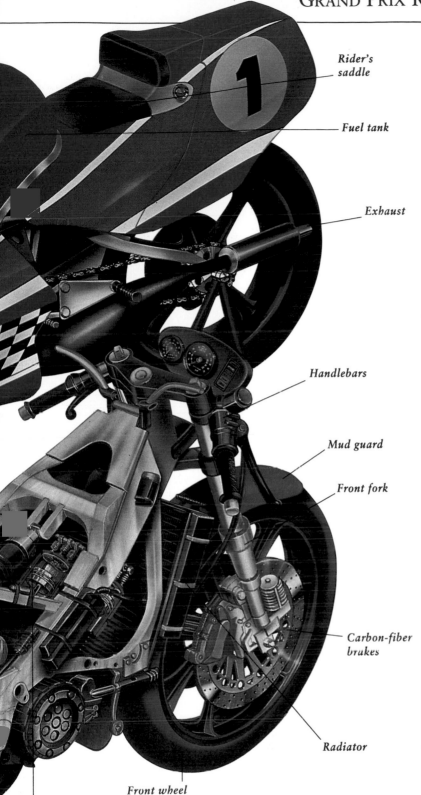

Rider's saddle

Fuel tank

Exhaust

Handlebars

Mud guard

Front fork

Carbon-fiber brakes

Radiator

Front wheel

GRAND PRIX START

GRAND PRIX RACING championships are held in a number of classes, each for different sizes of engine. These range from 125 cc (7.6 cubic inches) to 250 cc (15.2 cubic inches) and 500 cc (30.5 cubic inches). The most powerful Grand Prix racing bikes can reach nearly 187 mph (300 km/h)!

There is also a Superbike class. Here the bikes either have 750-cc (46-cubic-inch), four-cylinder engines or 1,000-cc (61-cubic-inch), two-cylinder engines. However, racing rules say that Superbikes must closely resemble road-going models. As such, their performance is not as good as the Grand Prix racing bikes – Superbikes can only reach speeds of about 163 mph (260 km/h).

ENGINE

The engine of a 500-cc (30.5-cubic-inch) Grand Prix bike will sometimes have four cylinders (right) arranged in a "V." When working at 13,000 rpm, the engine produces up to 170 bhp – more than three times the average car – to power a vehicle that is only one-fifth the weight.

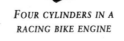

FOUR CYLINDERS IN A RACING BIKE ENGINE

TWO-WHEELED SPEED

The 1920s saw the world of motorcycling enter a golden age. Companies, such as Norton and Indian, started to build cheaper and more powerful machines for both racing and normal use. The American ACE Motorcycle Company made bikes powered by massive four-cylinder engines. In 1923, one of their models, a specially-tuned ACE XP-4 (below) ridden by Red Wolverton, established a world motorcycle land-speed record of 130 mph (210 km/h).

HUSQVARNA V-TWIN

The Swedish Husqvarna company produced 350-cc (21-cubic-inch) and 500-cc (31.5-cubic-inch) motorcycles that were successful in road racing during the 1920s and 1930s. The 500-cc (31.5-cubic-inch) model (below) was capable of 118 mph (190 km/h). Today, the company makes bikes for scrambling and speedway.

HUSQVARNA V-TWIN

MOTORCYCLE LAND-SPEED RECORDS

In the quest for greater and greater speed, motorcycle builders came up with more novel ways to cut through the air. One attempt in 1938 attached a streamlined body around a Brough Superior motorcycle.

STREAMLINED BROUGH SUPERIOR

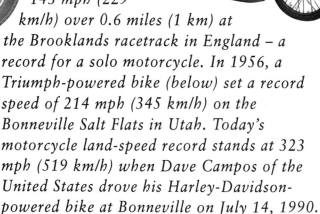

Ridden by E.C. Fernihough (right), the bike achieved 143 mph (229 km/h) over 0.6 miles (1 km) at the Brooklands racetrack in England – a record for a solo motorcycle. In 1956, a Triumph-powered bike (below) set a record speed of 214 mph (345 km/h) on the Bonneville Salt Flats in Utah. Today's motorcycle land-speed record stands at 323 mph (519 km/h) when Dave Campos of the United States drove his Harley-Davidson-powered bike at Bonneville on July 14, 1990.

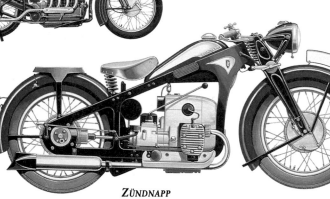

ZÜNDNAPP

ZÜNDNAPP

The 1935 Zündnapp (above) was fitted with a 500-cc (30.5-cubic in), two-cylinder engine. One unusual feature of the bike was the shift stick on one side of the engine. This was used to change gears in the same way as a car. The bike also had a hinged rear mudguard to make it easier to change the rear wheel.

TRIUMPH RECORD BREAKER

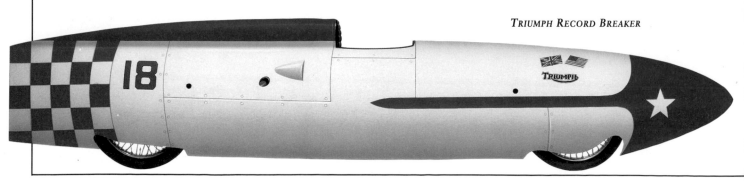

THE NORTON PITS DURING A TT RACE

JAPANESE SUPERBIKES

Today the most powerful road bikes in the world are produced by Japanese companies. The ultimate prize goes to the Honda CBR1100XX Super Blackbird (below). This powerful machine has a 1,137-cc (69-cubic-inch), four-cylinder engine that can produce 162 bhp. This can accelerate the machine from 0–60 mph (0–96 km/h) in a staggering 2.5 seconds (as fast as a Formula One racing car). The bike has a top speed of 188 mph (300 km/h)!

THE TT RACES

The Isle of Man TT (Tourist Trophy) was first run in 1907. The race snakes its way through the hilly countryside of the island. Early races were dominated by British-built Norton bikes (above and below). Today's TT bikes record speeds of about 123 mph (198 km/h), completing each lap of the route in a little over 18 minutes.

HONDA CBR1100XX SUPER BLACKBIRD

DRAG BIKES

The fastest drag bikes (below) can cover 0.25 miles (0.4 km) in about 6.5 seconds! During a run these bikes can reach speeds of 205 mph (328 km/h). The engines in these amazing machines produce as much power as the fastest production cars, such as the Jaguar XJ220 (see page 7), but the machines themselves weigh only half as much. The result is an acceleration from 0-60 mph (0-96 km/h) in a little under one second!

NORTON BIKE AT ISLE OF MAN TT RACE

DRAG BIKE

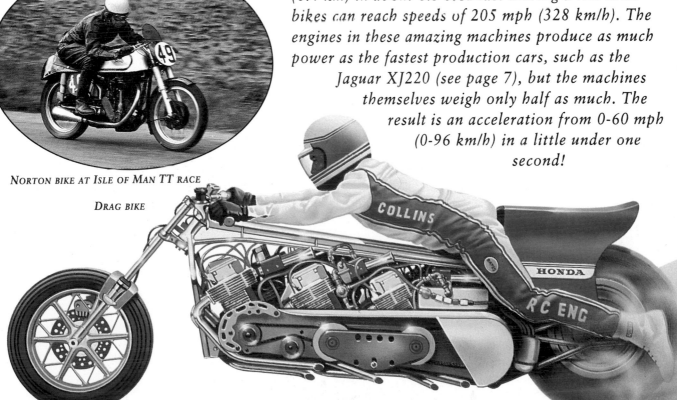

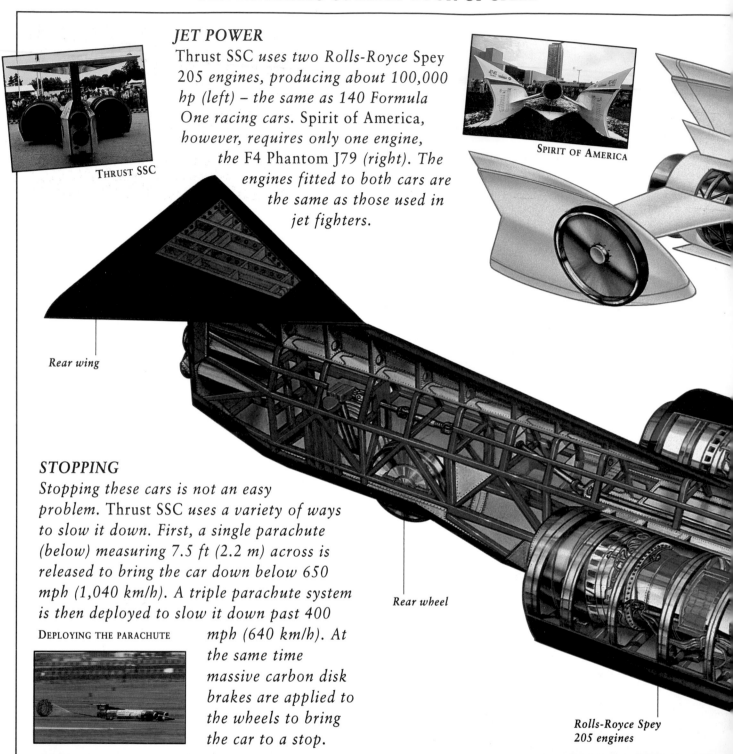

JET POWER

Thrust SSC *uses two Rolls-Royce Spey 205 engines, producing about 100,000 hp (left) – the same as 140 Formula One racing cars. Spirit of America, however, requires only one engine, the F4 Phantom J79 (right). The engines fitted to both cars are the same as those used in jet fighters.*

THRUST SSC

SPIRIT OF AMERICA

Rear wing

STOPPING

Stopping these cars is not an easy problem. Thrust SSC *uses a variety of ways to slow it down. First, a single parachute (below) measuring 7.5 ft (2.2 m) across is released to bring the car down below 650 mph (1,040 km/h). A triple parachute system is then deployed to slow it down past 400 mph (640 km/h). At the same time massive carbon disk brakes are applied to the wheels to bring the car to a stop.*

DEPLOYING THE PARACHUTE

Rear wheel

Rolls-Royce Spey
205 engines

ALTHOUGH THE SOUND BARRIER has been broken by aircraft, it has yet to be achieved by ground-based vehicles. But two cars are attempting to go beyond the speed of sound, which is 750 mph (1,200km/h) at sea level: the *Spirit of America* driven by American Craig Breedlove and *Thrust SSC* driven by former British fighter pilot Andrew Green. Unfortunately, both cars have run into trouble. *Thrust SSC* has been dogged by poor weather, while technical difficulties have led to a postponement of *Spirit of America*'s attempt.

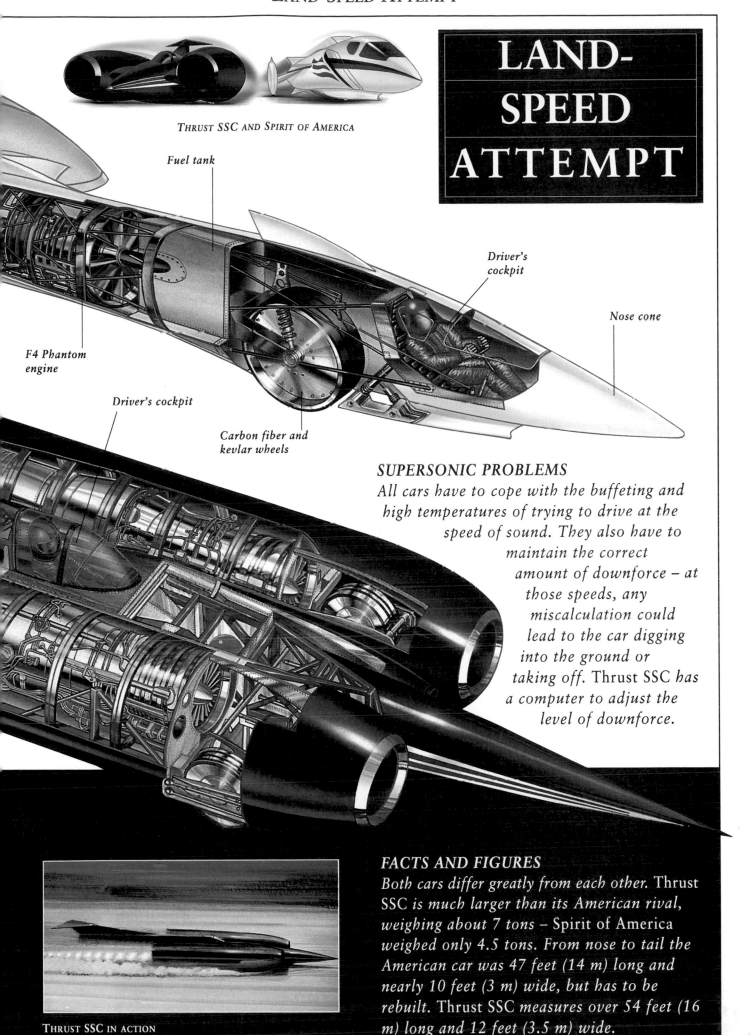

LAND-SPEED ATTEMPT

THRUST SSC AND SPIRIT OF AMERICA

Fuel tank

Driver's cockpit

Nose cone

F4 Phantom engine

Driver's cockpit

Carbon fiber and kevlar wheels

SUPERSONIC PROBLEMS
All cars have to cope with the buffeting and high temperatures of trying to drive at the speed of sound. They also have to maintain the correct amount of downforce – at those speeds, any miscalculation could lead to the car digging into the ground or taking off. Thrust SSC has a computer to adjust the level of downforce.

FACTS AND FIGURES
Both cars differ greatly from each other. Thrust SSC is much larger than its American rival, weighing about 7 tons – Spirit of America weighed only 4.5 tons. From nose to tail the American car was 47 feet (14 m) long and nearly 10 feet (3 m) wide, but has to be rebuilt. Thrust SSC measures over 54 feet (16 m) long and 12 feet (3.5 m) wide.

THRUST SSC IN ACTION

FORMER RECORD HOLDERS

RESURRECTED CAR

John Parry Thomas steered his Higham Special called "Babs" (below) to a record speed of 170 mph (272 km/h) in April 1926. A year later he tried to regain the record that had since been broken by Malcolm Campbell (see below). Sadly, Babs crashed on this attempt, killing the driver. As a mark of respect, the car was buried. Fifty years later, Babs has since been "resurrected" and restored to sit in a museum.

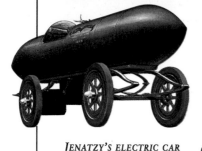

JENATZY'S ELECTRIC CAR

"BABS"

The quest for the land-speed record has led to the creation of some unique cars. The first record holders were either electric- or steam-powered vehicles. One of these electric cars, driven by Frenchman Camille Jenatzy (above), broke the record in 1899, reaching 66 mph (105 km/h). However, it wasn't long before gasoline-driven cars asserted their supremacy. The Ford 999 (below) was fitted with a 100-cubic in (1.6-liter) gasoline engine. In 1904, Henry Ford himself drove the car across the frozen ice of Lake Saint Clair to a record-breaking speed of 91 mph (147 km/h).

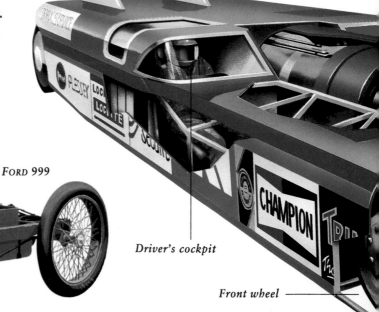

Rear fin

FORD 999

Driver's cockpit

Front wheel

SPEED KINGS

One of the greatest drivers between the WWI and WWII was Sir Malcolm Campbell, who held the land-speed record no fewer than nine times – he also held the water-speed record at the same time! All the cars (and boats) he drove were named Bluebird. One car, driven in 1933 (right), took the record to 273 mph (436.8 km/h). His son Donald continued the tradition of naming his vehicles Bluebird. In 1964, his car powered by a Proteus gas turbine (below) engine set a new land-speed record of 403 mph (644.96 km/h).

1964 BLUEBIRD

1933 BLUEBIRD

THUNDERBOLT AND RAILTON

Two drivers, George Eyston and John Cobb, dominated the world of land-speed records during the years before and after World War II. Driving the Thunderbolt, an enormous car powered by two Rolls-Royce engines, Eyston pushed the record to 357.5 mph (572 km/h) in 1939. Cobb had to wait eight years before mounting another attempt. His Napier Railton (left) broke the record, reaching 394 mph (631 km/h).

NAPIER
RAILTON

SPIRIT OF AMERICA

One of the great speed-record drivers in the last thirty years has been Craig Breedlove. Driving his cars, he has broken the record several times. The first happened in 1964, when he steered Spirit of America – Sonic One (right), a three-wheeled jet powered car, to 526 mph (847 km/h). Since then he has pushed the record to 601 mph (961 km/h) in 1965. His latest attempt, also called Spirit of America, is trying to break the speed of sound (see pages 18-19).

Rolls-Royce
Avon 302 **engine**

THRUST 2

THRUST 2

On October 4, 1983, Richard Noble drove Thrust 2 (left) to set a new land-speed record in the Black Rock Desert in Nevada. The car, designed by John Ackroyd, was built around a Rolls-Royce Avon 302 jet engine used in RAF fighter aircraft. Producing 16,000 lb (7,700 kg) of thrust, it powered the car to 633 mph (1,019 km/h). Had it gone 6 mph (10 km/h), the car would have generated enough lift to take off – with disastrous results!

SPIRIT OF
AMERICA-
SONIC 1

Air intake

THE BLUE
FLAME

THE BLUE FLAME

Gary Gabelich steered this rocket-powered car to a speed of 631 mph (1,016 km/h) on October 23, 1970, breaking the previous land-speed record. Even though the record was broken by Thrust 2 (see above), The Blue Flame (right) still remains the fastest rocket-car.

SPEED ON THE WATER

As trading routes stretched to the very corners of the Earth, a need arose for fast boats to carry cargoes as quickly as possible. The Clipper (left) was a fast, slender sailing vessel that was developed in the mid-1800s. The name comes from the way the ships "clipped off" the miles on their journey. Clippers could travel nearly 470 miles (750 km) in 24 hours and could cross the Atlantic in as little as 12 days. One of the most famous clippers was the Cutty Sark, which now sits in dry dock in Greenwich, London.

CLIPPER UNDER FULL SAIL

TURBINIA

At the presentation of the British navy to Queen Victoria during her Diamond Jubilee year of 1897, a small boat appeared from nowhere and raced amongst the battleships. The boat was Turbinia (above), designed by the British engineer Sir Charles Parsons. It was fitted with three steam turbines, each turning a propeller. These drove the boat to a speed of 34.5 knots (63.8 km/h), which was incredibly fast for the turn of the century.

WATER WINGS

When traveling at low speeds, a hydrofoil looks just like a normal boat. However, as its speed increases, the boat lifts out of the water, exposing a set of wings underneath the hull. The hydrofoil's wings work by creating less pressure above the wing than underneath (below), pushing the wing up and the boat with it. Because less of the boat is in contact with the water, friction along the whole hull is reduced, and the hydrofoil can travel at speeds much greater than a normal boat. Typical hydrofoils can travel between 30-55 knots (56-102 km/h), but experimental craft have reached speeds of more than 80 knots (148 km/h)!

Less pressure above the wing

Water wing

More pressure above the wing

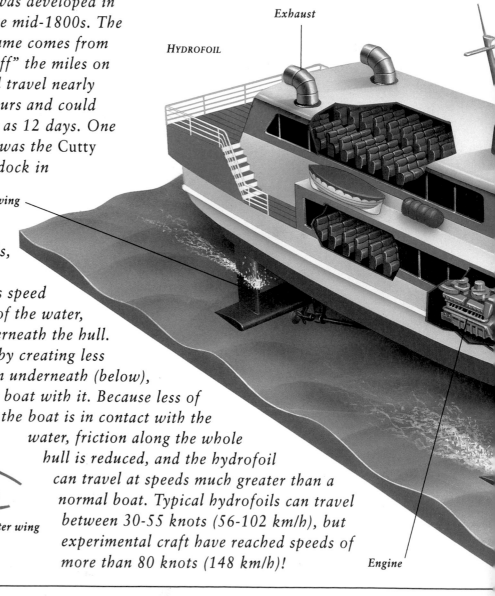

Exhaust

HYDROFOIL

Rear wing

Engine

WATER SPEED RECORDS

The water-speed record has been intensely fought over the years. In 1918, a hydrofoil designed by Alexander Graham Bell set a record of 61.6 knots (114 km/h). Today's official record was set by Kenneth Warby in 1978 and stands at 276 knots (511 km/h). He steered his hydroplane, Spirit of Australia (right), across Blowering Dam Lake in Australia. The boat is also said to have achieved 300 knots (555 km/h), but this could not be confirmed.

DONALD CAMPBELL AND THE FATAL CRASH IN BLUEBIRD

BLUEBIRD

Following in his father's footsteps (see page 20), Donald Campbell set records on both land and water. In 1964 he set a water speed record of 239 knots (442 km/h) in his boat Bluebird. Three years later he tried to break the 300-knot barrier. However, disaster struck when his boat crashed (above).

AMERICA'S CUP

The America's Cup is named after the yacht that won the trophy in 1851. Since then, the cup has been contested between the holders and a challenger every three or four years. Until 1983, yachts representing the United States won every time. In that year, the yacht Australia 2 took the trophy by winning the series, four races to three.

AMERICA'S CUP YACHTS

BLUE RIBAND

The Blue Riband, also called the Hales Trophy, is awarded to the fastest regular commercial crossing of the Atlantic. The current holder is the liner United States which, on its maiden voyage between the 3-7 of July 1952, averaged a speed of 35 knots (66 km/h). It sailed between the Ambrose Light vessel off America and the Bishop Rock lighthouse off Britain in 3 days, 10 hours, 40 minutes.

Front wing

THE UNITED STATES

SINGLE-HULLED POWERBOAT

OFFSHORE POWERBOAT racers are the speed-kings of the water world. The boats they use range from single-hulled vessels with v-shaped bottoms (above) to twin-hulled catamarans (main picture). These powerful boats plow through the open sea, around courses that may be over 250 miles (400 km) long.

CUSHION OF AIR

As a twin-hulled powerboat accelerates, the layer of air trapped in the tunnel between the two hulls is compressed. This lifts the boat,

RACING HYDROPLANES

reducing the amount of the vessel that is in contact with the water, reducing friction and increasing the speed that the boat can travel.

A similar effect occurs in hydroplanes (above). However, these smaller craft hardly touch the water. Instead, they skim, or "plane" across the water's surface on a cushion of trapped air.

TWIN-HULLED POWERBOAT

Aluminum hull

Races are between boats of the same engine size, that can range in power from 100 to 5,000 hp. The result is a speed of 120 knots (220 km/h) for the more powerful boats!

TAKING THE KNOCKS

Powerboat racing is a very tough sport for both boats and crews. This boat is over 50 feet (15 m) long and has to be strong enough to crash through waves that can be 25 feet (8 m) high. To cope with this, the hulls are made from hard-wearing aluminum.

INSIDE THE COCKPIT

The driver and the crew member sit one behind the other in a high-tech cockpit resembling that of a fighter jet. In some of the more powerful boats, this cockpit can be ejected clear of the boat should an accident occur.

The driver at the front keeps the boat on the right course using electronic navigation systems while the other crew member controls the throttle (which controls the engine speed). Each wears a "kill-switch," which is a cord attached to the boat that stops the boat if the crew are thrown clear.

THE POWER-BOAT

Throttle controller

Driver

Rear wing

Propeller

Exhaust

Fuel tank

POWERBOAT ENGINES

This powerboat has two 500-cubic-inch (8.2-liter), V-12 Lamborghini engines, positioned in each of the boat's hulls. These incredibly powerful engines can accelerate the boat from 0 to 85 knots (0 to 160 km/h) in under four seconds. To achieve this, the propellers are sent spinning at up to 10,000 rpm, each throwing up a plume of water, or "roostertail" that is 110 ft (30 m) long.

GAS GUZZLERS

The two hulls of the catamaran hold the enormous fuel tanks. The engines need a lot of fuel – during a race they can get through about 40 gallons (180 liters) every hour. Fuel is pumped between the two tanks to ensure that the boat stays perfectly balanced.

POWERBOAT IN ACTION

INTO THE SKY

GB
Sportster
R-1

In the quest for air supremacy, World War I saw the development of ever faster aircraft. The Spad 13 (below) was powered by an Hispano-Suiza V-8 engine which pushed the plane to 130 mph (210 km/h), making it one of the fastest planes of the conflict.

SPAD 13

GB SPORTSTER

The period between the two world wars saw an increasing interest in flying, especially in races. The GB Sportster R-1 (above) was one of the most successful racing planes of its day. It won the Thompson Trophy Race in 1932 and set a new plane-speed record of 296 mph (477 km/h). The tiny plane consisted of a small body fitted behind a huge engine. The R-1's career ended in 1933 when it flipped upside-down and crashed during a race.

SUPERMARINE S6B

The French arms manufacturer, Jacques Schneider, began a competition in 1913 to encourage the development of marine aviation – planes that took off and landed on water with the use of floats. Anyone who won the competition three times in a row would win the trophy outright. This happened in 1931, when the British company

SUPERMARINE *S6B*

Supermarine entered the S6B (left and right). It won the race and the Schneider Trophy, flying at 340 mph (548 km/h). The information gathered by the S6B led to the creation of the Spitfire fighter aircraft of World War II.

SUPERMARINE
S6B

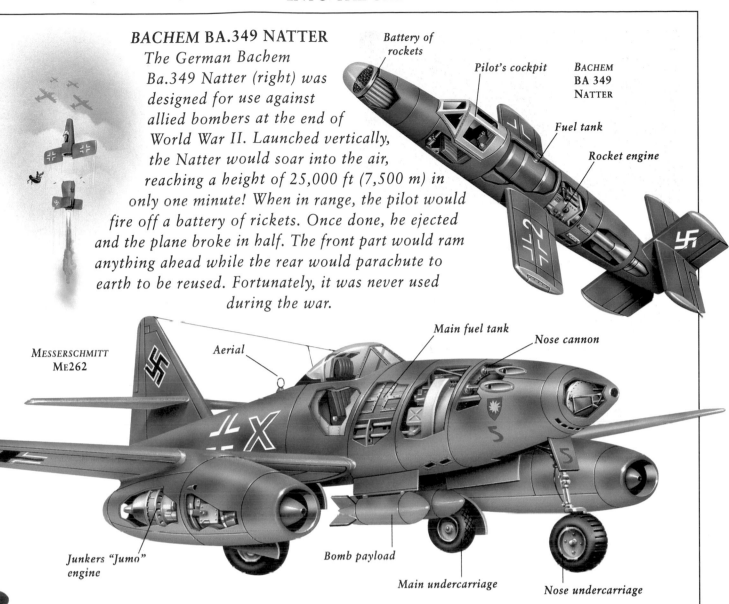

BACHEM BA.349 NATTER

The German Bachem Ba.349 Natter (right) was designed for use against allied bombers at the end of World War II. Launched vertically, the Natter would soar into the air, reaching a height of 25,000 ft (7,500 m) in only one minute! When in range, the pilot would fire off a battery of rickets. Once done, he ejected and the plane broke in half. The front part would ram anything ahead while the rear would parachute to earth to be reused. Fortunately, it was never used during the war.

Battery of rockets

Pilot's cockpit

BACHEM BA 349 NATTER

Fuel tank

Rocket engine

MESSERSCHMITT ME262

Aerial

Main fuel tank

Nose cannon

Junkers "Jumo" engine

Bomb payload

Main undercarriage

Nose undercarriage

BIRTH OF THE JET AIRCRAFT

The idea for a jet-powered aircraft was first patented by English pilot Sir Frank Whittle in the 1930s. However, it was not until the arrival of the Messerschmitt Me262 (above) in 1944 that a jet aircraft entered service in World War II. It could fly at 538 mph (866 km/h) and its overall performance was far superior to allied jets that arrived soon after, such as the Gloster Meteor (below). Despite this, the Me262 was built too late and in too few numbers to alter the course of the war.

P-51 MUSTANG

GLOSTER METEOR

NORTH AMERICAN P-51 MUSTANG

The Mustang (above) was fitted with a Rolls-Royce Merlin engine that could push it to 487 mph (784 km/h) making it one of the fastest propeller-driven aircraft of World War II. The ease with which it could be flown earned it the nickname "the Cadillac of the skies."

S P E E D
IN THE
A I R

SUPERSONIC FIRSTS

When it first flew in 1953, the North American F-100 Super Saber (main picture) brought combat aircraft into the supersonic age. This single-seater

CONVAIR B-58 HUSTLER

fighter could reach 864 mph (1,390 km/h), or Mach 1.31. The Convair B-58 Hustler (above) first flew in 1956. It was the first bomber to go beyond Mach 1 and also the first to reach Mach 2. Its maximum speed was 1,385 mph (2,215 km/h), or Mach 2.1.

TU-95/142 "BEAR"

T*oday's skies are filled with incredibly fast aircraft. Since the end of World War II, the majority of these planes have been jet-powered, sometimes traveling at speeds far beyond the sound barrier. However, many airlines still use propeller aircraft for short flights, while armed forces still have transport and reconnaissance planes, such as the Russian Tu-95/142 "Bear" (above). It is capable of flying at 575 mph (925 km/h), or Mach 0.82, making it the fastest propeller-driven aircraft.*

Pratt and Whitney
J-57 engine

Auxiliary fuel tank

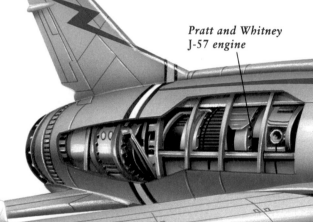

CONCORDE *AND* CONCORDSKI

The 1960s saw the development of the first two supersonic passenger aircraft – Concorde and the Tupolev Tu-144 (below). Both aircraft could fly at more than twice the speed of sound.

PANAVANIA TORNADO

SWINGING WINGS

Several planes use swinging wings to aid their performance, sweeping them forward for slow flight and back for fast flight (right). These include the F-111 and the Tornado (above). The latter can sweep its wings back from 23° to 67° and some versions can fly at 1,500 mph (2,414 km/h) or Mach 2.27.

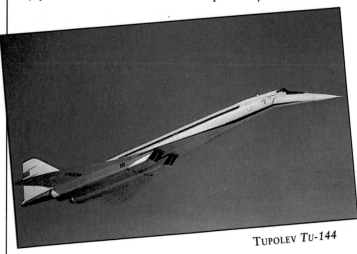

TUPOLEV TU-144

"BLACKBIRD"

The Lockheed SR-71 "Blackbird" (right) is the fastest jet-powered aircraft in the world. Powered by two Pratt and Whitney turbo-ramjet engines, the aircraft is capable of reaching 2,193 mph (3,529.56 km/h) or Mach 3.35. It can fly to the very edge of the atmosphere – a height of 100,000 ft (30,000 m)! Today, several Blackbird's have been given to NASA. These are being used for research into the next generation of supersonic aircraft (see pages 36-37).

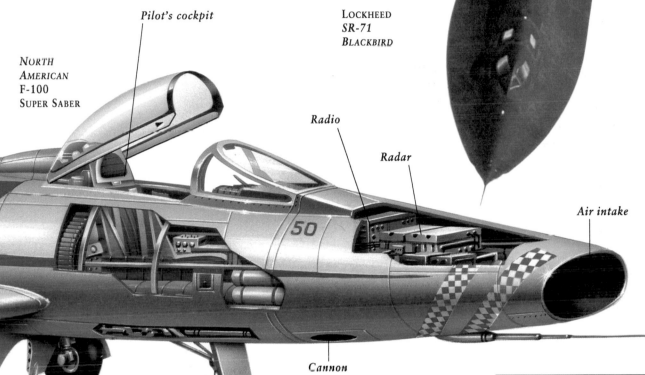

LOCKHEED
SR-71
BLACKBIRD

NORTH
AMERICAN
F-100
SUPER SABER

Pilot's cockpit

Radio

Radar

Air intake

Cannon

Nose undercarriage

JETS OF THE FUTURE

Aircraft designers are always looking for ways to increase an aircraft's speed or maneuverability. This has led to the development of some unusual looking aircraft,

EUROFIGHTER

such as the Eurofighter (above) and the YF-22, the experimental version of the F-22 Lightning 2 (left). The Eurofighter has small movable wings, or "canards." These allow it to perform maneuvers that normal aircraft would find impossible. The YF-22 uses "thrust vectoring" to help steer it. This system involves movable flaps over the exhausts. These flaps deflect the thrust, steering the plane through unconventional maneuvers. The plane can fly at 1,460 mph (2,335 km/h) or Mach 2.2.

YF-22 IN FLIGHT

THE MIG-31 FOXHOUND

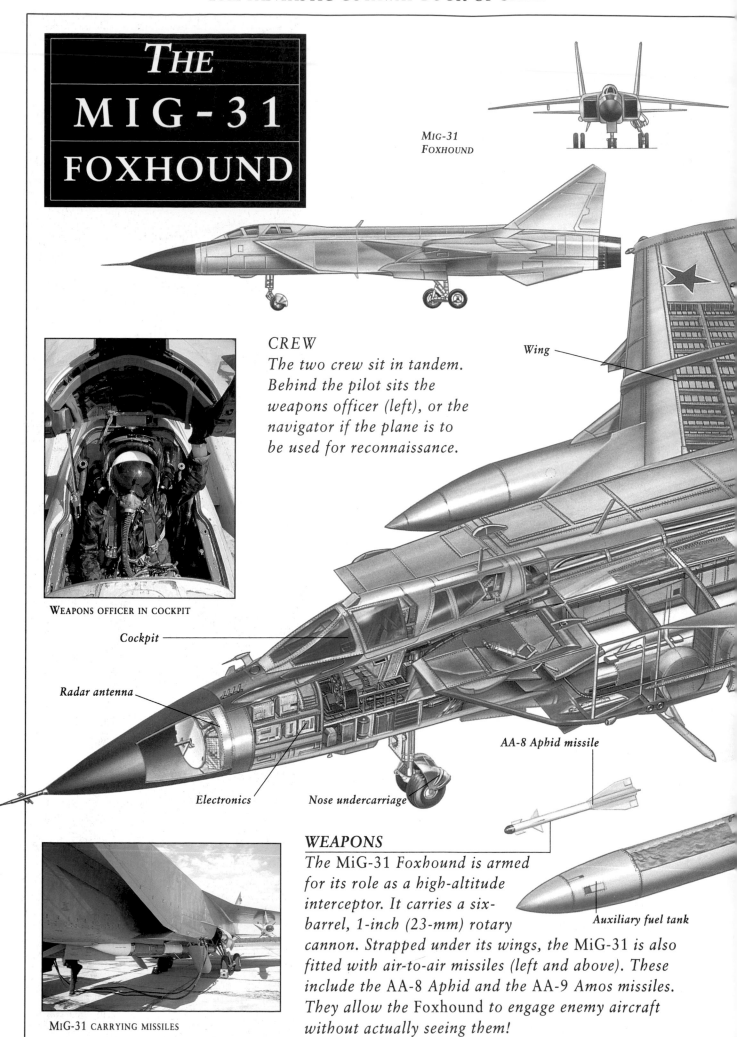

MIG-31
FOXHOUND

CREW
The two crew sit in tandem.
Behind the pilot sits the
weapons officer (left), or the
navigator if the plane is to
be used for reconnaissance.

Wing

WEAPONS OFFICER IN COCKPIT

Cockpit

Radar antenna

Electronics

Nose undercarriage

AA-8 Aphid missile

WEAPONS
The MiG-31 Foxhound is armed
for its role as a high-altitude
interceptor. It carries a six-
barrel, 1-inch (23-mm) rotary
cannon. Strapped under its wings, the MiG-31 is also
fitted with air-to-air missiles (left and above). These
include the AA-8 Aphid and the AA-9 Amos missiles.
They allow the Foxhound to engage enemy aircraft
without actually seeing them!

Auxiliary fuel tank

MIG-31 CARRYING MISSILES

POWER PLANT

The MiG-31 Foxhound is powered by two Perm D-30F6 afterburning turbofans. Air for these is sucked through two air intakes and blasted out through the two exhausts creating the massive thrust needed to push it to its maximum speed.

Jet nozzle

Tail fin

MIG-31 DEPLOYING BRAKING PARACHUTE

CAPABLE OF FLYING at a staggering 1,875 mph (3,000 km/h), or Mach 2.83, the *MiG-31 Foxhound* is the fastest jet fighter in the world. The aircraft was designed purely to fly high and fast, capable of soaring to altitudes of up to 67,600 ft (20,600 m). From here it can engage an enemy aircraft quickly and at distance without the need to operate in close combat (see left).

Alternatively, with all of its weapons removed the Foxhound can act as a super-fast reconnaissance plane, flying quickly over enemy positions and monitoring them.

AA-9 Amos missile

AFTERBURNERS

An afterburner is situated between the turbine and the exhaust nozzle of a jet engine. When gases leave the turbine they are still rich in oxygen. The afterburner injects more fuel into these gases and ignites them, raising the temperature greatly. These hotter gases accelerate through the nozzle, increasing the amount of thrust for short periods.

THE X-PLANES

CHUCK YEAGER

*A*fter World War II, the newly formed NACA (which later became NASA) started the X-planes – a program of experimental planes to extend the performance of aircraft in general. The first X-plane, the Bell X-1 (below), was flown by Chuck Yeager (left) on October 14, 1947 to a speed of 670 mph (1,078 km/h), becoming the first aircraft to fly faster than the speed of sound.

DOUGLAS X-3

DOUGLAS X-3
The X-3 (left) was a single-seat jet aircraft with a slim body and a tapered nose. During its flying career between 1952 and 1955 it was used to test the suitability of its dagger-like shape at speeds around the sound barrier.

BELL X-5
Flown between 1951 and 1954, the X-5 (below) was the first aircraft that could sweep its wings while it was in flight. The wings could be swept back to 60°, allowing it to perform better at higher speeds, particularly when it approached the speed of sound. The X-5 led to the development of aircraft such as the Tornado (see page 28).

BELL X-1

BELL X-5

MARTIN X-24A
The X-24A (below) was part of a project looking into "lifting bodies" – aircraft that use their fuselage to provide lift and so do not need wings. The X-24A flew at speeds up to 1,060 mph (1,696 km/h) or Mach 1.6 reaching an altitude of 71,825 ft (21,765 m).

MARTIN X-24B
The X-24B (below) achieved a speed of 1,166 mph (1,865 km/h) or Mach 1.76 and an altitude of 97,350 ft (29,500 m). It made its final powered flight in September 1975. Information collected by all of NASA's lifting bodies, such as the X-24A and X-24 B, was used to build the Space Shuttle.

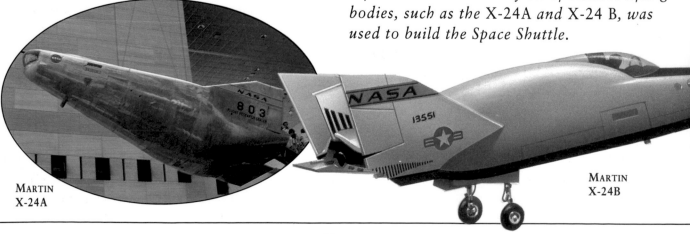

MARTIN X-24A

MARTIN X-24B

ROCKWELL X-31

The X-31 (right) was developed to examine how thrust vectoring and movable canards (see page 29) can be used together to create a highly maneuverable aircraft. As a result, the X-31 has been able to fly horizontally with its nose pointed up at an angle of 70° – a maneuver conventional aircraft would find impossible. In terms of its performance, the X-31 can fly at speeds of up to 848 mph (1,357 km/ h) or Mach 1.28 and to an altitude of 40,000 feet (12,200 m).

ROCKWELL X-31

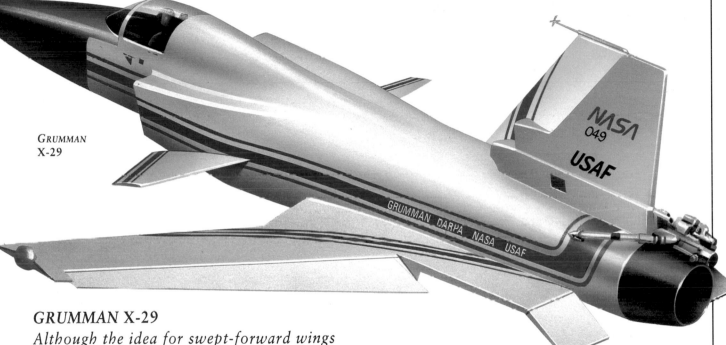

GRUMMAN X-29

GRUMMAN X-29

Although the idea for swept-forward wings is not new (it was first thought up during World War II, but the technology was lacking to build one), the X-29 (above) is still a revolutionary aircraft.

The design of the wings makes the aircraft very maneuverable. However, it also makes the X-29 very unstable. To overcome this, computers continuously monitor the aircraft and stop it from crashing. The aircraft also looked into the use of advanced materials in the construction of the body. The Grumman X-29 first flew in December 1984, and since then achieved a maximum speed of 1060 mph (1,696 km/h) or Mach 1.6 and reached an altitude of 50,000 ft (15,150 m).

X-36

The X-36 (below) is an unorthodox-looking plane, lacking a tailplane which conventional aircraft use to help them turn. Instead, the X-36 will use thrust vectoring and movable canards to steer the aircraft (see page 29).

The X-36 will also be one of the first planes where full-size prototypes will not be built. Instead, one-quarter scale models will be flown by remote control using pilots safely on the ground in virtual reality cockpits.

X-36

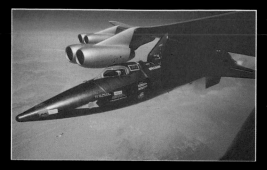

X-15 UNDER THE WING OF A *B-52*

FIRST FLOWN IN 1959, the *X-15* proved an invaluable research aircraft for NASA in its development of the reusable space shuttle. Rather than waste precious fuel on takeoff under its own power, the *X-15* was launched in the air from a flying *B-52* bomber (above). After its launch, the aircraft would climb rapidly to test the effects of flight at heights up to 67 miles (107 km) above the Earth's surface – some *X-15* pilots qualified for astronaut's wings!

Alternatively, the *X-15* would burn its fuel to reach astonishing speeds – up to 4,520 mph (7,232 km/h), or Mach 6.7!

AIRCRAFT DIMENSIONS

The X-15 measured 53 feet (16 m) from nose to tail and had a wingspan of 22 feet (6.7 m). It was shaped like a missile with a wedge-shaped tail and thin,

stubby wings. When launched, it weighed on average about 34,000 lbs (15,500 kg), depending on the mission. Over half of this weight was made up by the liquid oxygen and anhydrous ammonia propellant needed to fuel the rocket – turning the aircraft into a virtual flying fuel tank!

EJECTOR SEAT

The ejector seat for the X-15 (left) was designed to save the pilot at supersonic speeds. Rockets would blast the pilot clear, before several parachutes slowed the descent, bringing the pilot safely to the ground.

FLIGHT CONTROLS

Within the atmosphere, the X-15 was controlled conventionally using flaps and rudders on the wings and tailplane. However, above 120,000 feet (36,000 m) the air is too thin to allow adequate control – the plane was virtually flying through space. As such, the plane has eight small thrust rockets, with which the pilot can control the position of the aircraft as it flies through the upper atmosphere.

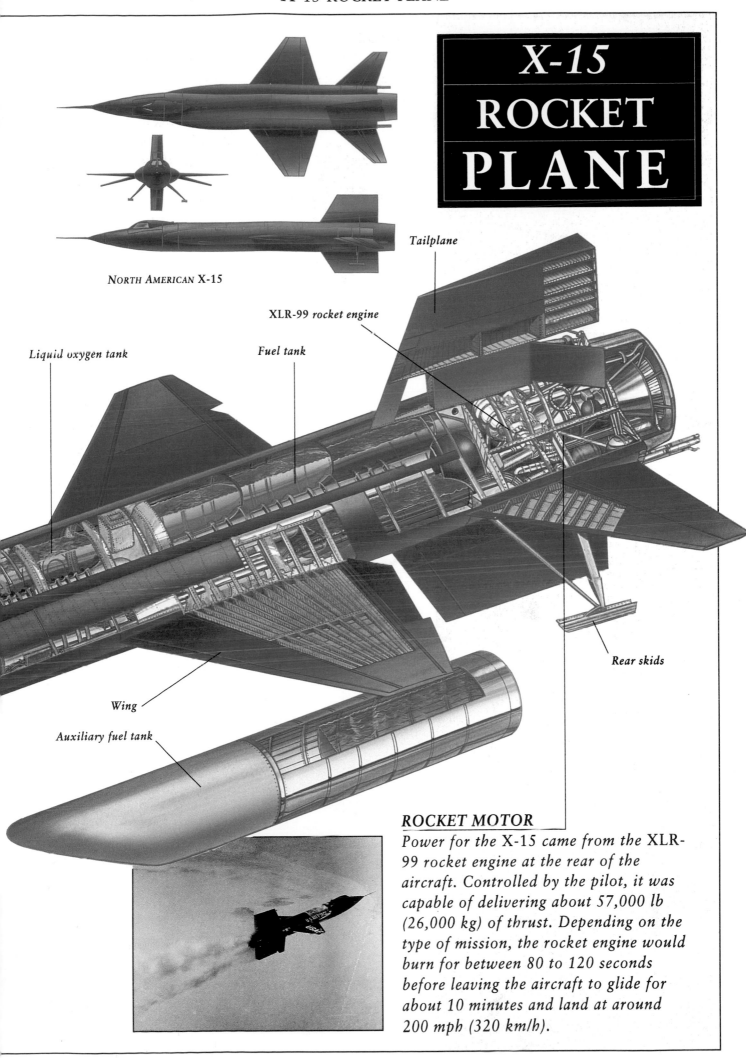

X-15 ROCKET PLANE

NORTH AMERICAN X-15

Tailplane

XLR-99 rocket engine

Liquid oxygen tank

Fuel tank

Rear skids

Wing

Auxiliary fuel tank

ROCKET MOTOR

Power for the X-15 came from the XLR-99 rocket engine at the rear of the aircraft. Controlled by the pilot, it was capable of delivering about 57,000 lb (26,000 kg) of thrust. Depending on the type of mission, the rocket engine would burn for between 80 to 120 seconds before leaving the aircraft to glide for about 10 minutes and land at around 200 mph (320 km/h).

THE NASP

NASP

HIGH FLIER

The proposed National Aero-Space Plane (NASP) would be able to carry passengers or satellites at incredible speeds. At these speeds and heights it must fly at, the NASP has to endure temperatures of 3,270°F because of friction with the outside air while flying at an altitude of 47.4 miles (76.3 km)! The wedge-shaped fuselage uses research from the X-plane lifting bodies (see page 32).

Oxygen tanks

Satellite payload

Hydrogen tanks

Nose undercarriage

Cockpit

FUSELAGE AND FUEL

At very high altitudes a normal air-breathing engine would be useless – there simply is not enough oxygen to keep the fuel burning. As such, the NASP will carry hydrogen in a special "slush" state as well as liquid oxygen.

The existing supersonic transport aircraft, *Concorde* and the Tupolev *Tu-144* (see page 28), are nearly 30 years old and in need of being replaced. Successors are being developed by Aérospatiale, British Aerospace, Boeing and Lockheed Martin. The new proposed "children of *Concorde*" will have speeds in excess of Mach 2 and be able to carry 300 people up to 6,250 miles (10,000 km). One other suggestion under study is for a plane that could cross the Earth in a couple of hours by flying into the upper atmosphere. At these

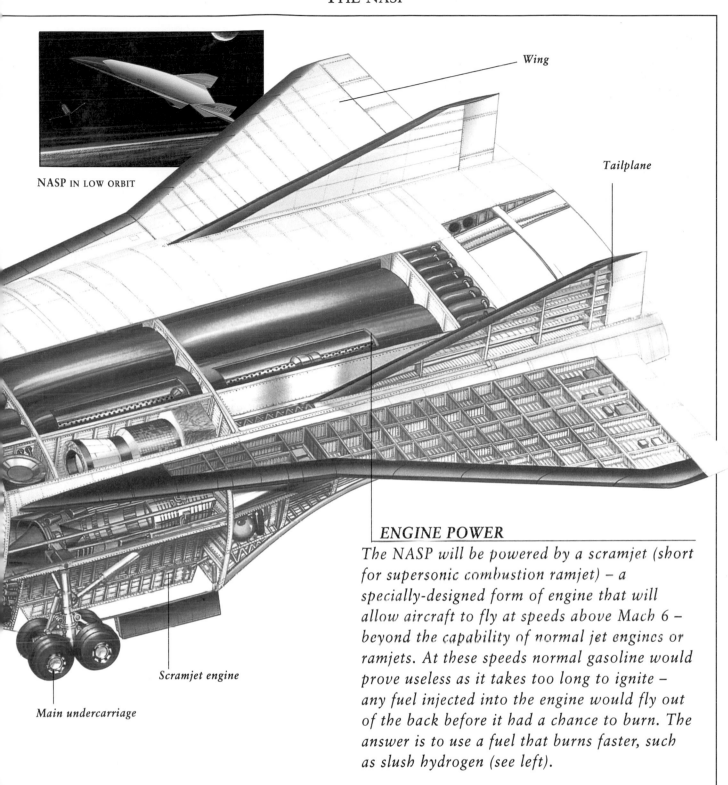

NASP IN LOW ORBIT

Wing

Tailplane

Scramjet engine

Main undercarriage

ENGINE POWER

The NASP will be powered by a scramjet (short for supersonic combustion ramjet) – a specially-designed form of engine that will allow aircraft to fly at speeds above Mach 6 – beyond the capability of normal jet engines or ramjets. At these speeds normal gasoline would prove useless as it takes too long to ignite – any fuel injected into the engine would fly out of the back before it had a chance to burn. The answer is to use a fuel that burns faster, such as slush hydrogen (see left).

heights, frictional forces are lower because there is very little air. This would allow the aircraft to fly faster than at lower altitudes. Once in the upper atmosphere, the aircraft could, in theory, fly at astonishing speeds – anything up to 16,560 mph (26,500 km/h) or Mach 25!

PROPOSED SUCCESSOR TO CONCORDE

GLOSSARY

Aerodynamics
The study of how easily a vehicle moves through a fluid, such as air or water.

Afterburner
The device found in some jet engines that injects extra fuel into the engine and reignites the exhaust gases to produce a massive increase in thrust.

Altitude
The height above the Earth's surface.

Chassis
Supporting framework for the body of a vehicle such as a car.

Cylinder
A hollow chamber found in engines in which a piston slides back and forth.

Downforce
The aerodynamically-produced downward force on a car that improves roadhandling.

Engine
The device that turns energy into force or motion. An internal combustion engine, such as a gasoline or diesel engine, converts energy generated inside its cylinder into motion.

Knot
The unit used to measure a boat's speed. One nautical mile per hour. A nautical mile is equivalent to 1.152 miles (1.853 km).

Lift
The aerodynamically-produced force made by a wing as it passes through a fluid. This raises a plane into the air and a hydrofoil boat out of the water.

Piston
A disk or cylinder that fits tightly within a cylinder and moves back and forth. In a steam engine the piston is moved by steam pressure; in an internal combustion engine it is moved by pressure from hot gases resulting from the combustion of fuel.

Propellant
The substance that is burned in a rocket or a jet engine to produce thrust.

Propeller
A device with several angled blades that rotates to propel a ship or an aircraft.

Shock absorber
The device that absorbs sudden shocks to the suspension of vehicles.

Speed of sound
The speed at which sound travels through the air. At an altitude of 39,600 feet (12,000 m), this is 662.5 mph (1,060 km/h). A Mach number is given to speeds in relation to the speed of sound. Hence, a plane flying at Mach 2 is flying at twice the speed of sound. Speeds above Mach 1 are called supersonic.

Supercharger
A device containing a fan driven by mechanical linkage from an engine. This blows air under pressure into the engine inlet to boost its power.

Thrust
The force generated by a jet or rocket engine that pushes a vehicle along.

Turbine
A device with a central shaft fitted with vanes so that when a liquid or gas, such as water or steam, flows over the vanes, the shaft rotates.

Turbocharger
A device containing a fan driven by a turbine that is turned by exhaust gases from engine. This blows air under pressure into the engine inlet to boost its power.

CHRONOLOGY

1897 *Turbinia* makes its appearance during a review of the British Royal Navy by Queen Victoria.

1899 Camille Jenatzy sets a new land-speed record, driving his steam-powered car to 66 mph (105 km/h).

1904 Henry Ford sets new land-speed record of 91 mph (147 km/h) driving a Ford 999.

1906 First Grand Prix held in France. It was won by Ferenc Szisz driving a Renault.

1907 First Isle of Man TT races held.

1911 First Monte Carlo rally held. It was won by Rougier, who drove from Paris in a *Turcat-Méry*.
First Indianapolis "500" held. It was won by R. Harroun and C. Patscke in a Marmon.

1923 First 24-hour race held at Le Mans. It was won by A. Lagache and R. Leonard, driving a Chenard-Walcker. Red Wolverton sets a motorcycle-speed record of 130 mph (210km/h).

1927 John Parry Thomas is killed trying to regain the land-speed record.

1931 The Supermarine *S6B* wins the Schneider Trophy, flying at a speed of 340 mph (548 km/h).

1935 Sir Malcolm Campbell sets the last of his land-speed records. He drives *Bluebird* to a speed of 301 mph (485 km/h).

1944 The Messerschmitt *Me262*, one of the first jet-powered aircraft, enters service with the Lutwaffe.

1947 Chuck Yeager becomes the first man to break the sound barrier, flying the Bell *X-1* to a specd of 670 mph (1,078 km/h).

1950 The first Formula One car race is held at Silverstone racing circuit. It was won by Giuseppe Farina driving an Alfa Romeo.

1952 The liner, the *United States*, wins the Blue Riband for setting the quickest commercial crossing of the Atlantic. It averaged a speed of 35 knots (66 km/h).

1964 Donald Campbell sets a new land-speed record of 403 mph (649 km/h) in his gas turbine driven *Bluebird*. Craig Breedlove sets the first of his land-speed records, pushing the speed to 469 mph (754 km/h) in his three-wheeled *Spirit of America*.

1966 W.J. Knight pilots the *North American X-15* to a speed of 4,534 mph (7,297 km/h) or Mach 6.7.

1967 Donald Campbell is killed trying to set a new water-speed record.

1969 *Concorde* becomes the first supersonic airliner to enter service. It can fly at speeds up to 1,450 mph (2,333 km/h) or Mach 2.2.

1970 The rocket-powered *Blue Flame* sets a new land-speed record. Driven by Gary Gabelich, it reaches 622 mph (1,002 km/h). It still remains a record for a rocket-powered car.

1976 Captain Eldon Joersz and Major George Morgan set a new air-speed record for a jet aircraft of 2193 mph (3,530 km/h) or Mach 3.35 flying a Lockheed *SR-71 Blackbird*.

1978 Kenneth Warby sets a new water-speed record of 276 knots (511 km/h) in the *Spirit of Australia*.

1983 Richard Noble steers the jet-powered *Thrust 2* to a new land-speed record, reaching 633 mph (1,019 km/h).

1985 Robert Barber breaks the 79-year-old record for a steam-powered car. His vehicle, *Steamin' Demon*, reaches 146 mph (234 km/h).

1990 Dave Campos sets a new motorcycle-speed record of 323 mph (519 km/h).

1996-7 Teams led by Craig Breedlove and Richard Noble attempt to break the land-speed record and the speed of sound with their cars the *Spirit of America* and *Thrust SSC*.

INDEX

Photographic credits:

Abbreviations: t-top, m-middle, b-bottom, r-right, l-left

Pages 4, 5 both, 7tl & br, 10 both, 11ml & mr, 12, 13b, 14m, 15, 18tl & tr, 19b, 23m, 24 both, 25, 27bl, 28br, 29 all & 32 t – Rex Features. 6t, 7tr, m & bl, 8 both, 9, 11tl & tr, 13t, 14b, 18b, 30 both & 31 – Frank Spooner Pictures. 11b – British Film Institute. 16m, 17t & b, 22tl, 23t & inset, 23b & 27br – Hulton Getty Collection. 17m – Honda UK. 22tr – Mary Evans Picture Library. 26 both, 28tl, tr & bl, 32ml, mr & b, 32, 34tr 35b & 37t – The Aviation Picture Library. 34tl – Rockwell Aerospace. 37b – British Aerospace.